W9-APD-077

Replacement costs will be
billed after 42 days overdue.

FRANKLIN PARK PUBLIC LIBRARY
FRANKLIN PARK, ILL.

L I F E   O F

SHOUTY

GOOD HABITS

edited by H. H. Ricks

RIXKIN

Published in 2010 by Rixkin, Atlanta. All rights reserved. This book cannot be reproduced, stored in a database, or transmitted via mechanical, electronic, recording, photocopying, or any means without prior written permission of both the copyright owner and the publisher.

Educators and librarians, for lesson plans and talking points, visit www.rixkin.com/resources

Rixkin books are available at discount pricing with quantity purchase for educational, business, fundraising, or sales promotional use.

Rixkin and the colophon are trademarks of Rixkin LLC.

Library of Congress Control Number: 2009908866

ISBN-13: 978-0-9842069-0-2
ISBN-10: 0-9842069-0-6

10 9 8 7 6 5 4 3 2 1
Printed in China

RIXKIN

Rixkin LLC
PO Box 11922
Atlanta, GA 30355
www.rixkin.com

Dedication

This book is dedicated to my father, my hero.
Thank you for believing in me.

●

Acknowledgements

Google
Lois Ricks
Jessie Reider
Willie Sanchez
Adobe Illustrator
Hoyland W. Ricks
Violet Travis Ricks
Prolong Printing Ltd.
Hoylande Young Failey
George Barr McCutcheon
Francis W. Parker School
The Buckhead Library
Wacom Co., Ltd.

When Shouty was young, a man gave him advice:
"Practice good habits the rest of your life."

Those words were heard, but not taken to heart.

His primary goal was whatever felt good.
Focus and planning? If only he would!

He preferred to relax, and chill-out instead—
Watching TV from the comfort of bed.

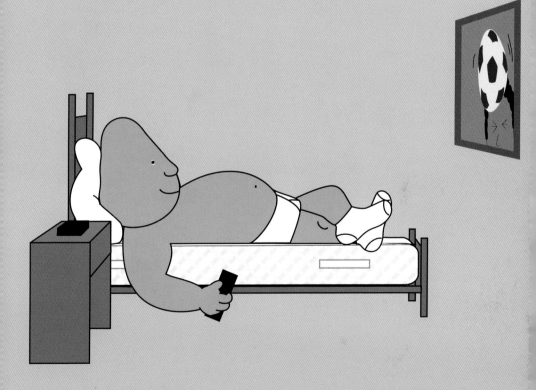

Too lazy to floss—his gums in bad shape.

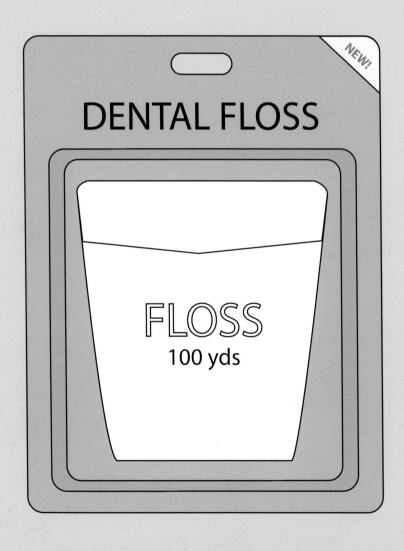

His room was a mess and his bills were late.

He read no books, but had seen every game.

His lawn looked so bad even he was ashamed.

Priorities? Please! "I'll do it tomorrow."

APRIL

MOW LAWN!

3 Do laundry ~~Record game~~ Renew license	**4** Laundry Wrap Cousin's birthday gift ~~Get new jersey~~ ~~Call about cable~~ Renew license

5 * Cousin's bday
Laundry
Wrap Cousin's gift
Pay Julian back
Renew license (DUE TODAY)

10 LAUNDRY!!!!
~~Wrap Cousin's gift~~
~~Pay Julian back~~
Work on tax return

11 ~~Buy underwear~~
Laundry
Work on taxes
~~Watch game at Leon's~~

12 Laundry
Work on taxes
~~Pick up movie~~
Renew license! ASAP!

17 Laundry
File for a tax extension
~~Renew license~~
(#HfBH-H)

18 ~~Laundry~~
File tax extension

~~Record game~~
File extension!!
~~Organize fant~~
~~football league~~
Exchange Cou
gift (get XL)

~~...SION!24~~

25 ~~Game at Leon's~~
~~Exchange Cousin's~~

FILE EXTENS
Exchange Co
gift

Life overwhelmed him like Kilimanjaro.

An effort was made, but the pull was great.
Bad habits teased and lured him with bait.

Depressed though he was about his sad plight,
He would not surrender without a good fight.

"I have this great vision of who I could be!
As I look in the mirror, that's not what I see."

Though he wanted success and to be first-rate,
He'd start, then quit, and procrastinate.

For the first time in months, from what we can tell—
He scrubbed, wiped, and waxed to a fare-thee-well,

But bad habits called in soothing tones,
And when that failed, used megaphones.

The couch said, "Relax today."
His stomach asked, "Is food on the way?"
His mind said, "I don't want to think!"
His throat asked, "Can you let me drink?"

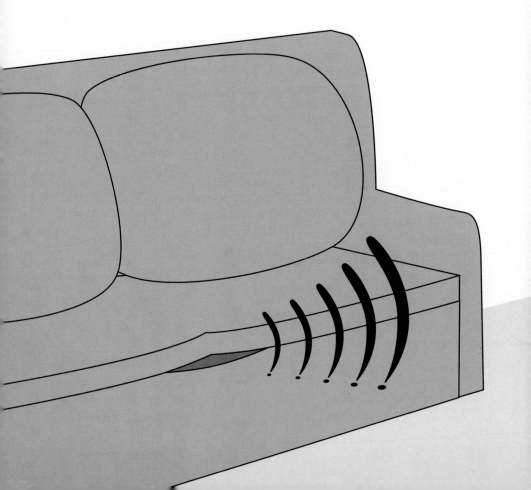

Will Shouty listen and miss what's in store?

Or refuse to give in to this tug-of-war?

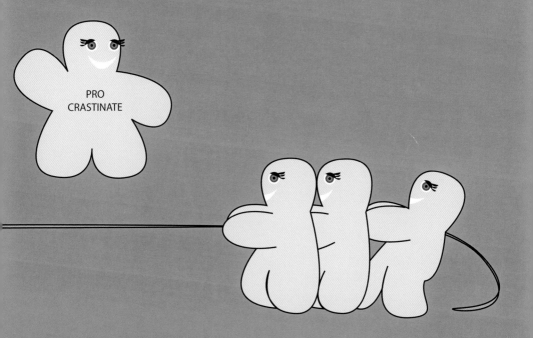

"Now I see what that wise man was saying.
I should have been focused, instead I was playing.

Time that was wasted I'll never get back.
How grateful am I to be on the right track!"

Hoping to leave old patterns behind,

Negative thoughts Shouty cleared from his mind.

A list of goals he viewed each day.

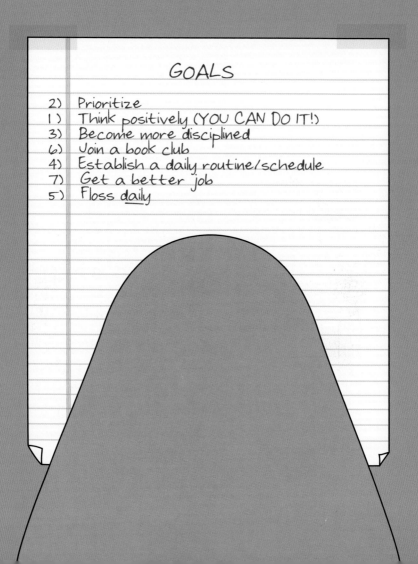

Shouty Mack was on his way!